HOPE
IS A HANDFUL OF DREAMS

BY
JUNE DUTTON

ILLUSTRATIONS BY
SUSAN PERL

HOPE IS A HANDFUL OF DREAMS is more than a child's book. Susan Perl sees the world with refreshing directness and honesty which allows her to draw with a skill and humor that can be satiric for structured society but lyrical for all living things.

HOPE IS A HANDFUL OF DREAMS is the newest in a succession of books illustrated by SUSAN PERL, the artist famous for her adorable children and their whimsical animal friends, all of whom cavort happily through these pages.

Austrian-born Susie lives in New York City — her passion is cats. Her talent speaks for itself in this lovely new book.

JUNE DUTTON is the author of seven specialty cook books. She has a journalism background, and she currently lives in Sausalito, California.

Hope is a new beginning.

Hope is outstretched arms.

Hope is
a morning
prayer...
an evening
blessing.

Hope is...

a ringing phone.

Hope is the sweetness of poetry.

Hope is well-scrubbed boys and sweetly-groomed girls.

Hope is an unopened letter.

Hope is
a bird's
nest
building.

Hope is a single candle in the dark.

Hope is a full and luminous moon.

Hope is a cure
for sadness...
a mender of
broken hearts.

Hope is the warmth 'round a winter hearth.

Hope is a new friend.

Hope is a bend in the road.

Hope is a heart full of sharing.

Hope is
a tear
kissed away.

Hope is
a kiss
for the bride.

Hope is the start of a journey.

Hope is the steady rhythm of earthly life.

Hope is
a rainbow.

Hope is the serenity of silence... the comfort of night.

Hope is
the pursuit
of treasure.

Hope is shelter from the storm.

Hope is strength to persevere.

Hope is the night before Christmas.

Hope is a strong body.

Hope is
a handful
of dreams.

Hope is a new hairdo.

Hope is
the sky filled
with stars.

Hope is
an abundance
of blossoms.

Hope is ever-present protest.

Hope is a patient heart.

Hope is another hand in yours.

Hope is an inheritance of freedom.

Hope is curiosity.

Hope is a healthy appetite.

Hope is the constancy of the tides.

Hope is a small gold ring.

Hope is new life.

Hope is an open door.

Hope is good smells

...from the kitchen.

Hope is a heart full of love.

Hope is what helps to make your garden grow.

Hope is
a feast
for
the spirit.

Hope is a hot cup of soup.

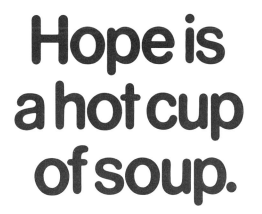

Hope is a cold glass

of milk.

Hope is
the first snowfall.

Hope is...

all baby things.

Hope is a penny in a wishing well.

Hope is a word of encouragement... a glance of reassurance.

Hope is
a full sail.

Hope is gentle humor... joyous laughter.

Hope is one's namesake.

Hope is everywhere.

Hope is
an adventure.

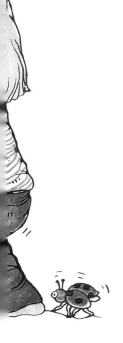

Hope is
a song.

Hope is
a mother's love.

Hope is applause.

Hope is the scent of lilacs... the buzz of a bee.

Hope is a fresh new morning.

Hope is the answer.

Hope is forever.